ALSO BY GUY A. ZONA

The House of the Heart Is Never Full
And Other Proverbs of Africa

▲ ▲ ▲ ▲ ▲ ▲ ▲ ▲ ▲ ▲ ▲ ▲ ▲ ▲ ▲ ▲

A TOUCHSTONE BOOK

Published by Simon & Schuster

GUY A. ZONA

▼▼▼▼▼▼▼▼▼▼▼▼▼▼▼

THE SOUL WOULD HAVE NO RAINBOW IF THE EYES HAD NO TEARS

▲▲▲▲▲▲▲▲▲▲▲▲▲▲▲▲▲

And Other Native American Proverbs

TOUCHSTONE
Rockefeller Center
1230 Avenue of the Americas
New York, New York 10020

TOUCHSTONE and colophon are registered
trademarks of Simon & Schuster Inc.

Designed by Pei Loi Koay
Manufactured in the United States of America

29   30   28

Library of Congress Cataloging-in-Publication
Data is available.

ISBN 0-671-79730-1

ACKNOWLEDGMENTS

The author is indebted to the following individuals and organizations for their contributions to this collection:

The American Indian Heritage Foundation

The American Indian Lore Association

Blue Cloud Abbey

Chief Serpent's Tail

Chief Standing Bear

The Council for Indian Education

Eastern Shawnee Tribe

Eastern Shoshone Cultural and Resource Center

Pride Runs Deep

P R E F A C E

Proverbs are time-honored truths which condense the collected wisdom and experience of a people and their culture. If you want to know a people, the saying goes, know their proverbs.

Proverbs often serve as a means of instruction in the rules of conduct and ethical behavior expected by all members of a society; what makes them an effective tool is that they are based on a keen observation of human nature and behavior rather than an idealized and unrealistic standard.

The proverbs collected in *The Soul Would Have No Rainbow If the Eyes Had No Tears* are those of people who love the land and regard it as sacred, who see daily prayer as a duty, and have no need to set apart one day in seven as a

With all things and in all things,
we are relatives.

(S I O U X)

▲ ▲ ▲

Stand in the light when you want
to speak out.

(C R O W)

▲ ▲ ▲

Life is both giving and receiving.

(M O H A W K)

▲ ▲ ▲

I seek strength, not to be greater
than my brother, but to fight my
greatest enemy—myself.

(*TRIBE UNKNOWN*)

▲ ▲ ▲

All children of Earth will be welcome
at our council fires.

(*SENECA*)

▲ ▲ ▲

Good and evil cannot dwell together
in the same heart, so a good man ought
not to go into evil company.

(D E L A W A R E)

▲ ▲ ▲

Know that we are eager to share our gifts,
in the name of love.

(S E N E C A)

▲ ▲ ▲

He who is present at a wrongdoing
and does not lift a hand to prevent it
is as guilty as the wrongdoers.

(O M A H A)

▲　▲　▲

Give me knowledge, so I may have
kindness for all.

(P L A I N S   I N D I A N)

▲　▲　▲

Treachery darkens the chain
of friendship, but truth makes
it brighter than ever.

(C O N E S T O G A)

▲ ▲ ▲

Before eating, always take a little
time to thank the food.

(A R A P A H O)

▲ ▲ ▲

Speak the truth in humility
to all people. Only then can you be
a true man.

(S I O U X)

▲ ▲ ▲

Truth does not happen,
it just is.

(H O P I)

▲ ▲ ▲

Sin is not allowed in God's tepee.

(M O H A W K)

▲ ▲ ▲

Lying is a great shame.

(S I O U X)

▲ ▲ ▲

Stolen food never satisfies hunger.

(O M A H A)

▲ ▲ ▲

Thoughts are like arrows:
once released, they strike their mark.
Guard them well or one day you may
be your own victim.

(N A V A J O)

▲ ▲ ▲

Respect the gift and the giver.

(O M A H A)

▲ ▲ ▲

Give your host a little something
when you leave; little presents are
little courtesies and never
offend.

(S E N E C A)

▲ ▲ ▲

I love a people who do not live
for the love of money.

(D U W A M I S H)

▲ ▲ ▲

When we show our respect for
other living things, they respond
with respect for us.

(A R A P A H O)

▲ ▲ ▲

It is less of a problem to be poor
than to be dishonest.

(A N I S H I N A B E)

▲ ▲ ▲

Even when we lay down,
we lay down on our own
path of life.

(P A W N E E)

▲ ▲ ▲

A good man does not take what belongs
to someone else.

(P U E B L O)

▲ ▲ ▲

Ask questions from your heart
and you will be answered
from the heart.

(O M A H A)

Judge not by the eye but
by the heart.

(C H E Y E N N E)

Easy money breeds indolence.

(A R A P A H O)

▲ ▲ ▲

Be kind to everything that lives.

(O M A H A)

▲ ▲ ▲

No one else can represent
your conscience.

(A N I S H I N A B E)

▲ ▲ ▲

To gossip is like playing checkers
with an evil spirit: you win occasionally
but are more often trapped at
your own game.

(H O P I)

▲ ▲ ▲

The rain falls on the just and the unjust.

(H O P I)

▲ ▲ ▲

Do not speak of evil
for it creates curiosity in the
hearts of the young.

(*L A K O T A*)

▲ ▲ ▲

Let no one speak ill of the absent.

(*H O P I*)

▲ ▲ ▲

Those who have one foot
in the canoe and one foot in the boat
are going to fall into the river.

(T U S C A R O R A)

▲ ▲ ▲

Always assume your guest is tired, cold,
and hungry, and act accordingly.

(N A V A H O)

▲ ▲ ▲

Love one another and do not strive
for another's undoing.

(S E N E C A)

▲ ▲ ▲

We will be known forever by
the tracks we leave.

(D A K O T A)

▲ ▲ ▲

Never sit while your seniors stand.

(C R E E)

▲ ▲ ▲

29

Even as you desire good treatment,
so render it.

(SENECA)

▲ ▲ ▲

Who serves his fellows is of all the greatest.

(DAKOTA)

▲ ▲ ▲

If you dig a pit for me, you dig
one for yourself.

(CREOLE)

▲ ▲ ▲

Listening to a liar is like
drinking warm water.

(T R I B E   U N K N O W N)

▲ ▲ ▲

An angry word is like striking
with a knife.

(H O P I)

▲ ▲ ▲

Each person is his own judge.

(P I M A)

▲ ▲ ▲

Do not judge your neighbor
until you walk two moons
in his moccasins.

(NORTHERN   CHEYENNE)

▲　▲　▲

One foe is too many and a hundred
friends too few.

(HOPI)

▲　▲　▲

Do not wrong or hate your neighbor,
for it is not he that you wrong
but yourself.

(P I M A)

▲ ▲ ▲

Many have fallen with the
bottle in their hand.

(L A K O T A)

▲ ▲ ▲

When a man prays one day and steals six,
the Great Spirit thunders and
the Evil One laughs.

(O K L A H O M A)

▲ ▲ ▲

Trouble follows sin as surely as
fever follows chill.

(H O P I)

▲ ▲ ▲

Let your eyes be offended
by the sight of lying and
deceitful men.

(H O P I)

The more you give, the more good
things come to you.

(C R O W)

Never interfere in a person's
decisions about what he will do
with his possessions.

(H O P I)

▲ ▲ ▲

The lazy man is apt to be envious.

(O M A H A)

▲ ▲ ▲

Man's law changes with his
understanding of man. Only the laws of the
spirit remain always the same.

(C R O W)

What the people believe is true.

(A N I S H I N A B E)

The Great Spirit has made us what we are:
it is not his will that we should be changed.
If it was his will, he would let us know;
if it is not his will, it would be wrong
for us to attempt it, nor could we,
by any art, change our nature.

(S E N E C A)

▲ ▲ ▲

Let your nature be known
and proclaimed.

(H U R O N)

▲ ▲ ▲

When a favor is shown to a white man,
he feels it in his head and the tongue speaks out;
when a kindness is shown to an Indian,
he feels it in his heart and the heart
has no tongue.

(SHOSHONE)

▲ ▲ ▲

Our pleasures are shallow,
our sorrows are deep.

(CHEYENNE)

▲ ▲ ▲

The song is very short because we
understand so much.

(N A V A J O)

I have been to the end of the earth.
I have been to the end of the waters.
I have been to the end of the sky.
I have been to the end of the mountains.
I have found none that are not my friends.

(N A V A J O)

If you see no reason
for giving thanks, the fault lies
in yourself.

(MINQUASS)

▲ ▲ ▲

An Indian, a partridge, and a spruce tree
cannot be tamed.

(CHEYENNE)

▲ ▲ ▲

First you are to think always of God.
Second you are to use all your powers
to care for your people and
especially for the poor.

(S I O U X)

▲　▲　▲

There is no death, only a change of worlds.

(D U W A M I S H)

▲　▲　▲

The only things that need the protection
of men are the things of men, not
the things of the spirit.

(CROW)

▲ ▲ ▲

All religions are but stepping stones
back to God.

(PAWNEE)

▲ ▲ ▲

The Great Spirit is not perfect: it has
a good side and a bad side. Sometimes
the bad side gives us more knowledge
than the good side.

(L A K O T A)

▲ ▲ ▲

The supreme law of the land is the Great Spirit's
law, not man's law.

(H O P I)

▲ ▲ ▲

44

The words of God are not like the oak
leaf which dies and falls to the earth, but
like the pine tree which stays
green forever.

▲　▲　▲

When the legends die, the dreams end;
there is no more greatness.

▲　▲　▲

We should be as water,
which is lower than all things yet stronger
even than the rocks.

(OGLALA SIOUX)

▲ ▲ ▲

One "Take this" is better than
two "I will give's."

(SOUTHWEST, UNKNOWN TRIBE)

▲ ▲ ▲

It makes no difference as to the name
of the God, since love is the real God
of all the world.

(A P A C H E)

▲ ▲ ▲

Not westward, but eastward seek the
coming of the light.

(D A K O T A)

▲ ▲ ▲

When we understand deeply in our hearts,
we will fear and love and know
the Great Spirit.

(OGLALA SIOUX)

▲ ▲ ▲

Everything the Power does,
it does in a circle.

(LAKOTA)

▲ ▲ ▲

The ones that matter most are
the children. They are the true
human beings.

(L A K O T A)

▲ ▲ ▲

If I am in harmony with my family,
that's success.

(U T E)

▲ ▲ ▲

Remember that your children are
not your own, but are lent to you
by the Creator.

(M O H A W K)

When an elder speaks, be
silent and listen.

(M O H A W K)

Never see an old person going
to carry water without getting a bucket
and going in their stead.

(T W A N A S)

A man or woman with many children
has many homes.

(L A K O T A)

Talk to your children while they
are eating; what you say will stay
even after you are gone.

(NEZ PERCE)

▲ ▲ ▲

Take your children with you where you go
and be not ashamed.

(HOPI)

▲ ▲ ▲

A child believes that only the
action of someone who is unfriendly
can cause pain.

(S A N T E E   S I O U X)

▲ ▲ ▲

You should water your children like
you water a tree.

(H O P I)

▲ ▲ ▲

When you die, you will be spoken of as
those in the sky, like the stars.

(Y U R O K)

▲ ▲ ▲

You are never justified in arguing.

(H O P I)

▲ ▲ ▲

Even your silence holds a sort of prayer.

(A P A C H E)

▲ ▲ ▲

It takes a whole village to raise a child.

(O M A H A)

Where there is true hospitality,
not many words are needed.

(A R A P A H O)

▲ ▲ ▲

Even in Paradise, living all alone
would be Hell.

(S E N E C A)

▲ ▲ ▲

Guard your tongue in youth, and in age you may mature a thought that will be of service to your people.

(S I O U X)

You can't get rich if you look after your relatives properly.

(N A V A J O)

▲ ▲ ▲

Don't walk behind me; I may not lead.
Don't walk in front of me; I may not follow.
Walk beside me that we may be as one.

(U T E)

▲ ▲ ▲

The good-looking boy may be
just good in the face.

(A P A C H E)

▲ ▲ ▲

See how the boy is with his sister
and you can know how the man will be
with your daughter.

▲ ▲ ▲

See your sons and daughters:
they are your future.

▲ ▲ ▲

The more you ask how far
you have to go, the longer your
journey seems.

(S E N E C A)

▲ ▲ ▲

Dreams are wiser than men.

(O M A H A)

▲ ▲ ▲

Creation is ongoing.

(L A K O T A)

▲ ▲ ▲

We stand somewhere between
the mountain and the ant.

(O N O N D A G A)

▲ ▲ ▲

Show respect for all men,
but grovel to none.

(S H A W N E E)

▲ ▲ ▲

There are no secrets. There is no mystery.
There is only common sense.

(O N O N D A G A)

▲　▲　▲

A spear is a big responsibility.

(N A V A J O)

▲　▲　▲

Hold fast to the words of
your ancestors.

(H O P I)

▲　▲　▲

The greatest strength is gentleness.

(I R O Q U O I S)

▲ ▲ ▲

There is no warning for
upcoming danger.

(C H E Y E N N E)

▲ ▲ ▲

When you see a rattlesnake poised
to strike, strike first.

(N A V A H O)

▲ ▲ ▲

Never go to sleep when your
meat is on the fire.

(P U E B L O)

▲ ▲ ▲

If we wonder often, the gift of
knowledge will come.

(A R A P A H O)

▲ ▲ ▲

No answer is also an answer.

(H O P I)

▲ ▲ ▲

You must live your life from
beginning to end; no one else
can do it for you.

(H O P I)

Don't let yesterday use up
too much of today.

(C H E R O K E E)

The pathway to glory is rough
and many gloomy hours
obscure it.

(C H I E F   B L A C K   H A W K)

▲ ▲ ▲

Pray to understand what
man has forgotten.

(L U M B E E)

▲ ▲ ▲

The soul would have no rainbow
if the eyes had no tears.

(M I N Q U A S S)

What is past and cannot be prevented
should not be grieved for.

(P A W N E E)

Knowledge that is not used is abused.

(C R E E)

Eating little and speaking little
can hurt no man.

(H O P I)

Every fire is the same size when it starts.

(S E N E C A)

One must learn from the bite of the fire
to leave it alone.

(S I O U X)

If a man is as wise as a serpent
he can afford to be as harmless
as a dove.

(*CHEYENNE*)

Misfortunes do not flourish on one path,
they grow everywhere.

(*PAWNEE*)

Beware of the man who
does not talk and the dog that
does not bark.

(CHEYENNE)

▲ ▲ ▲

Great men are usually destroyed by those
who are jealous of them.

(SIOUX)

▲ ▲ ▲

69

Better that one only should
suffer than that all should perish.

(O J I B W A)

The eyes of men speak words the tongue
cannot pronounce.

(C R O W)

It is easy to be brave from a safe distance.

(O M A H A)

Never help a person who doesn't
help anybody else.

(H O P I)

▲ ▲ ▲

Before you choose a counselor, watch him
with his neighbor's children.

(S I O U X)

▲ ▲ ▲

A danger foreseen is half-avoided.

(C H E Y E N N E)

▲ ▲ ▲

Poverty is a noose that strangles
humility and breeds disrespect
for God and man.

(S I O U X)

The frog does not drink up the pond
in which he lives.

(S I O U X)

Seek wisdom, not knowledge.
Knowledge is of the past, wisdom is
of the future.

(L U M B E E)

Force, no matter how concealed,
begets resistance.

(L A K O T A)

▲ ▲ ▲

Don't be afraid to cry.
It will free your mind of
sorrowful thoughts.

(H O P I)

A brave man dies but once—
a coward many times.

(I O W A)

Wisdom comes only when you stop
looking for it and start living the life
the Creator intended for you.

(HOPI)

In twenty-four hours, a louse
can become a patriarch.

(SENECA)

What should it matter that one bowl
is dark and the other pale, if each
is of good design and serves
its purpose well?

(*H O P I*)

The bird who has eaten cannot fly with
the bird that is hungry.

(*O M A H A*)

One rain won't make a crop.

(C R E O L E)

▲ ▲ ▲

One finger cannot lift a pebble.

(H O P I)

▲ ▲ ▲

The man who freely gives his opinion
should be ready to fight fiercely.

(I O W A)

▲ ▲ ▲

77

A rocky vineyard does not need
a prayer but a pickax.

(N A V A J O)

When a fox walks lame, the
old rabbit jumps.

(O K L A H O M A)

A starving man will eat with the wolf.

(O K L A H O M A)

▲ ▲ ▲

Seek the ways of the eagle,
not the wren.

(OMAHA)

▲ ▲ ▲

Those who do not fear God
are not strong.

(SENECA)

▲ ▲ ▲

A good soldier is a poor scout.

(CHEYENNE)

▲ ▲ ▲

The smarter a man is the more
he needs God to protect him from
thinking he knows everything.

(P I M A)

▲ ▲ ▲

There is nothing as eloquent as a
rattlesnake's tail.

(N A V A J O)

▲ ▲ ▲

Trouble no man about his religion—
respect him in his views and demand
that he respect yours.

(S H A W N E E)

▲ ▲ ▲

When you know a man, you know his
face but not his heart.

(S E N E C A)

▲ ▲ ▲

Each bird loves to hear himself sing.

(ARAPAHO)

▲ ▲ ▲

Our first teacher is our own heart.

(CHEYENNE)

▲ ▲ ▲

He who would do great things should not
attempt them all alone.

(SENECA)

▲ ▲ ▲

The way of the troublemaker is thorny.

(U M P Q U A)

▲ ▲ ▲

Man has responsibility, not power.

(T U S C A R O R A)

▲ ▲ ▲

You already possess everything necessary
to become great.

(C R O W)

▲ ▲ ▲

Most of us do not look as handsome
to others as we do to ourselves.

(A S S I N I B O I N E)

▲ ▲ ▲

The coward shoots with shut eyes.

(O K L A H O M A)

▲ ▲ ▲

A man must make his own arrows.

(W I N N E B A G O)

▲ ▲ ▲

To touch the earth is to have
harmony with nature.

(O G L A L A   S I O U X)

▲ ▲ ▲

We are made from Mother Earth and
we go back to Mother Earth.

(S H E N A N D O A H)

▲ ▲ ▲

Even animals have their taboos.

(N O R T H E R N   P L A I N S   I N D I A N)

▲ ▲ ▲

All plants are our brothers and sisters.
They talk to us and if we listen,
we can hear them.

(ARAPAHO)

Listen to the voice of nature, for it
holds treasures for you.

(HURON)

▲ ▲ ▲

If a man is to do something
more than human, he must have more
than human power.

▲ ▲ ▲

When man moves away from nature
his heart becomes hard.

▲ ▲ ▲

Take only what you need and leave
the land as you found it.

(A R A P A H O)

▲ ▲ ▲

The rainbow is a sign from Him
who is in all things.

(H O P I)

▲ ▲ ▲

God gives us each a song.

(U T E)

▲ ▲ ▲

All dreams spin out from
the same web.

(HOPI)

▲ ▲ ▲

Everyone who is successful must have
dreamed of something.

(MARICOPA)

▲ ▲ ▲

Cherish youth, but trust old age.

(PUEBLO)

▲ ▲ ▲

Old age is not as honorable as death,
but most people want it.

(C R O W)

The one who tells the stories
rules the world.

(H O P I)

In age, talk; in childhood, tears.

(H O P I)

A people without a history is like
the wind over buffalo grass.

(S I O U X)

▲ ▲ ▲

A people without faith in themselves
cannot survive.

(H O P I)

▲ ▲ ▲

Some are smart but they are not wise.

(S H O S H O N E)

▲ ▲ ▲

He who has great power should
use it lightly.

(SENECA)

▲ ▲ ▲

Great chiefs prove their worthiness.

(SENECA)

▲ ▲ ▲

White men have too many chiefs.

(NEZ PERCE)

▲ ▲ ▲

In death I am born.

(H O P I)

▲ ▲ ▲

They are not dead who live in the
hearts they leave behind.

(T U S C A R O R A)

▲ ▲ ▲

All who have died are equal.

(C O M A N C H E)

▲ ▲ ▲

A hungry stomach makes a short prayer.

(P A I U T E)

▲ ▲ ▲

The moon is not shamed by
the barking of dogs.

(S O U T H W E S T)

▲ ▲ ▲

Do not be envious of a gift that is
cheerfully given.

(O M A H A)

▲ ▲ ▲

Sing your death song and die like
a hero going home.

(S H A W N E E)

▲ ▲ ▲

Death always comes out of season.

(P A W N E E)

▲ ▲ ▲

Life is not separate from death.
It only looks that way.

(B L A C K F O O T)

▲ ▲ ▲

It is no longer good enough to cry peace,
we must act peace, live peace,
and live in peace.

(S H E N A N D O A H)

▲ ▲ ▲

How we fought for our country
is written in blood.

(D U W A M I S H)

▲ ▲ ▲

Make my enemy brave and strong,
so that if defeated, I will not
be ashamed.

(P L A I N S   I N D I A N)

▲ ▲ ▲

The weakness of the enemy
makes our strength.

(C H E R O K E E)

▲ ▲ ▲

Death is nothing and pain is nothing,
but cowardice is crime and disgrace
the greatest punishment.

(D A K O T A)

The Great Spirit is always angry with men
who shed innocent blood.

(I O W A)

There can never be peace between nations
until it is first known that true peace is
within the souls of men.

(O G L A L A   S I O U X)

▲ ▲ ▲

It is senseless to fight when you
cannot hope to win.

(A P A C H E)

▲ ▲ ▲

A sparrow in the bush is better than
a vulture flying.

(*B L A C K F O O T*)

▲ ▲ ▲

Even a small mouse has anger.

(*T R I B E   U N K N O W N*)

▲ ▲ ▲

Those that lie down with dogs
get up with fleas.

(*B L A C K F O O T*)

▲ ▲ ▲

There are many good moccasin tracks
along the trail of a straight arrow.

(F O X)

▲ ▲ ▲

After dark all cats are leopards.

(Z U N I)

▲ ▲ ▲

Not every sweet root gives birth
to sweet grass.

(T R I B E   U N K N O W N)

▲ ▲ ▲

Never part from the chiefs' path,
no matter how short or beautiful
the byway may be.

(SENECA)

A good chief gives,
he does not take.

(MOHAWK)

Work hard, keep the ceremonies,
live peaceably, and unite
your hearts.

(H O P I)

▲ ▲ ▲

Dreams count; the Spirits have pitied us
and guided us.

(C R E E)

▲ ▲ ▲

Never let things slide: keep a steady hold,
each one of you upon yourself—do not throw away
your life simply to spite another.

(C R E E)

▲ ▲ ▲

Only two relationships are possible—
to be a friend or to be an enemy.

(C R E E)

▲ ▲ ▲

Love yourself; get outside yourself
and take action. Focus on the solution;
be at peace.

(S I O U X)

▲ ▲ ▲

The dead add their strength and
counsel to the living.

(H O P I)

▲ ▲ ▲

Be satisfied with needs
instead of wants.

(T E N T O N   S I O U X)

▲ ▲ ▲

In this world the unseen has power.

(A P A C H E)

▲ ▲ ▲

Rituals must be performed with
good and pure hearts.

(H O P I)

▲ ▲ ▲

Mother Nature is always there to watch
and care for her own.

(K I O W A)

▲ ▲ ▲

Talk was given to the
people for good.

(S A U K)

▲ ▲ ▲

Deeds speak louder than words.

(A S S I N I B O I N E)

▲ ▲ ▲

When you lose the rhythm
of the drumbeat of God, you are lost
from the peace and rhythm of life.

(C H E Y E N N E)

▲ ▲ ▲

Inner peace and love are the greatest
of God's gifts.

(T E N T O N   S I O U X)

▲ ▲ ▲

You must always be careful with
something that is greater than
you are.

(SHOSHONE)

▲ ▲ ▲

We are all one child, spinning
through Mother Sky.

(SHAWNEE)

▲ ▲ ▲

Everything has a beginning.

(K I O W A)

▲ ▲ ▲

Every animal knows far more
than you do.

(N E Z   P E R C E)

▲ ▲ ▲

I am living in poverty,
but in peace.

(H O P I)

▲ ▲ ▲

It is good to be reminded that each of us
has a different dream.

(C R O W)

▲ ▲ ▲

Wishing cannot bring autumn glory
nor cause winter to cease.

(K I O W A)

▲ ▲ ▲

There is no fear where there is faith.

(K I O W A)

▲ ▲ ▲

Do not only point out the way,
but lead the way.

(*SIOUX*)

▲ ▲ ▲

Men in search of a myth will
usually find one.

(*PUEBLO*)

▲ ▲ ▲

God is pleased to hear children pray.

(*OSAGE*)

▲ ▲ ▲

Strive to be a person who is never absent
from an important act.

▲ ▲ ▲

It is good to tell one's heart.

▲ ▲ ▲

To go on a vision quest is to go into
the presence of the great mystery.

▲ ▲ ▲

Sometimes dreams are wiser
than waking.

(O G L A L A   S I O U X)

▲ ▲ ▲

We are friends; we must assist each other
to bear our burdens.

(O S A G E)

▲ ▲ ▲

Silence has so much meaning.

(Y U R O K)

▲ ▲ ▲

All things have inner meaning
and form and power.

(H O P I)

▲ ▲ ▲

Do not allow anger to poison you.

(H O P I)

▲ ▲ ▲

Teaching should come from within
instead of without.

(H O P I)

▲ ▲ ▲

Is it not better for one hundred to
pray for one than for one to pray
alone for himself?

(TENTON SIOUX)

▲ ▲ ▲

There are many paths to a meaningful
sense of the natural world.

(BLACKFOOT)

▲ ▲ ▲

Life is as the flash of the firefly
in the night, the breath of the
buffalo in winter time.

(B L A C K F O O T)

▲ ▲ ▲

Walk lightly in the spring; Mother Earth
is pregnant.

(K I O W A)

▲ ▲ ▲

There is a need for obedience
all around us.

(S A U K)

▲ ▲ ▲

Sharing and giving are the ways of God.

(S A U K)

▲ ▲ ▲

Let us continue to honor that which
remains only in dream memory.

(O N E I D A)

▲ ▲ ▲

God teaches the birds to make nests,
yet the nests of all birds are not alike.

(D U W A M I S H)

▲ ▲ ▲

When you have a talent of any kind,
use it, take care of it, guard it.

(S A U K)

▲ ▲ ▲

A shady lane breeds mud.

(H O P I)

▲ ▲ ▲

Always look at your moccasin
tracks first before you speak of
another's faults.

(S A U K)

Teachers not only teach, but they also learn.

(S A U K)

It is good for the living to perform
ceremonies for those who
have died.

(W I N N E B A G O)

▲ ▲ ▲

There is a hole at the end
of the thief's path.

(L A K O T A)

▲ ▲ ▲

Friendship cannot be bought;
you have to help make it.

(S A U K)

▲　▲　▲

When you have learned about love,
you have learned about God.

(F O X)

▲　▲　▲

Each person is his own judge.

(S H A W N E E)

▲　▲　▲

In anger a man becomes dangerous
to himself and to others.

(U M A H A)

▲   ▲   ▲

When the wisdomkeepers speak,
all should listen.

(S E N E C A)

▲   ▲   ▲

Words are the voice of the heart.

(T U S C A R O R A)

▲   ▲   ▲

When there is true hospitality,
not many words are needed.

(A R A P A H O)

▲ ▲ ▲

Be brave where bravery is honorable.

(A S S I N I B O I N E)

▲ ▲ ▲

Learn how to talk, then learn
how to teach.

(N E Z   P E R C E)

▲ ▲ ▲

One has to face fear or forever
run from it.

(C R O W)

▲ ▲ ▲

The grandfathers and the grandmothers
are in the children; teach them well.

(O J I B W A Y)

▲ ▲ ▲

Flowers are for our souls to enjoy.

(S I O U X)

▲ ▲ ▲

Misfortunes will happen to the wisest
and best of men.

(P A W N E E)

▲ ▲ ▲

The mark of shame does not
wash away.

(O M A H A)

▲ ▲ ▲

There are many ways to God.

(A R A P A H O)

▲ ▲ ▲

The wildcat does not make enemies
by rash action. He is observant, quiet,
and tactful, and he always
gains his ends.

(P A W N E E)

▲ ▲ ▲

The old days will never be again,
even as a man will never again
be a child.

(D A K O T A)

▲ ▲ ▲

Be an early riser: the game
does not snuggle their heads
on feather pillows.

(A S S I N I B O I N E)

▲ ▲ ▲

It is not good for anyone
to be alone.

(C H E Y E N N E)

▲ ▲ ▲